THE LITERARY MOSAIC

Poems & Stories from diverse voices

Compiled and edited by

Abhishek Thakkar

&

Purba Chakraborty

Published by

Notion Press

Compiler + Editor:

Abhishek Thakkar & Purba Chakraborty

Anthology (English)

In this book:

Dedicated to

Papa

(Mr. Sakti Pada Chakraborty),

his resilience and fighting spirit and all the donors of Papa's fundraiser for cancer treatment

If thou speakest not I will fill my heart with thy silence and endure it. I will keep still and wait like the night with starry vigil and its head bent low with patience.

The morning will surely come, the darkness will vanish, and thy voice pour down in golden streams breaking through the sky.

Then thy words will take wing in songs from every one of my birds' nests, and thy melodies will break forth in flowers in all my forest groves.

Rabindranath Tagore (Gitanjali)

Sun of Harij, Son of Amba

Abhishek Thakkar

A mind as spotless as Ganga
A heart as compassionate as Mother Earth
A soul as elevated as Swami Vivekananda

His mind absorbs the wisdom of Shankaracharya
and Krishna
His life embodies the teachings of Ramakrishna
Paramahansa

He chants loud and silently
He meditates unfailingly and unceasingly

He serves the Divine Mother with his endless love
He sees Shiva and Parvati in all living entities and
not just in the lokas above

He is detached like Shiva
He is devoted like Hanuman

He speaks only when it is necessary
He advises dhyan on Maa as the panacea for all the
worries

He reminded my father of the eternal and
indestructible nature of soul

He helped my father deal with the loss of his mother
by reminding him of the soul's oneness with the
Supersoul.

He served humanity as an English teacher and as a
spiritual master
He reminded all of us that only God/Goddess is the
Supreme Master

Countless souls bowed down to him and were
blessed by him
Anyone who walked into his home became joyful
and was no more grim

We used to touch his feet and ask him to bless us
with peace and prosperity
He gave us wealth of transcendental knowledge,
devotion and his humanity

O great soul, I wish I could sing hymns praising thy
sublime nature
O great soul, within you lies past, present and future

O Vyas Saheb, you like Maa Amba are eternal and
infinite
O Vyas Saheb, you are the Lighthouse and a
crescent moon in our gloomy night

Reside in my heart like Maa Sita and Shri Ram do
in Hanuman's heart
May I always remember you in each work I do from
its start.

The Brightest Star

(Dedicated to actor Sushant Singh Rajput)

Abhishek Thakkar

A gift of evolution,
A being who ushered in a revolution,
He fused science and spirituality.

An elevated soul,
A dreamer who saw the One in the whole,
He indefatigably served humanity.

A cognoscente of physics,
A maestro of his craft,
He embodied ingenuity and creativity.

A reader of human profoundness,
A seer of the future,
He bestowed meaning to mortality.

Haikus

Abhishek Vipul Thakkar

Haiku #1

Strength burns brightly,
Lone star against ebony sea,
Hope resurges.

Haiku #2

Golden streak hits leaf
Breeze dances atop warm sands
Earth breathes, soft and deep.

Haiku #3

The silence echoes,
The gate stays still and untouched,
You are no more here.

Haiku #4

Night ends its journey,
White light reaches us as gold,
You are born again.

About Abhishek Thakkar

Abhishek Thakkar is an author, teacher and an entrepreneur. He has authored 5 books till now and he is also a contributing author to more than 15 anthologies of poetry and short stories.

He has also contributed research articles, poems and book reviews in international journals and reputed magazines such as International Journal of English Language and Literature, The Literary Herald Journal and the LLP Magazine.

His latest book 'Age of Chaucer (BOOK 1)' is an academic e-book which is written specially for the students of English Literature.

He is the co-compiler and co-editor of 'The Language of Love' and 'The Language of Divinity" poetry books.

Journey

Purba Chakraborty

I gaze at the autumn sky with a newly fallen maple leaf in my hand. The graceful cumulus clouds, oblivious to my inner tempest, look at me and sigh. Then, they continue their play as I try to unknot the memories of one particular autumn afternoon. The more I unknot the memories, the more they get tangled and along with them, I get tangled too - a chaotic mess. I start writing on the yellow notebook to unburden my heart. My spilled thoughts are all over the yellow pages. Every day, I write a new story as I try to unknot the memories. I add a new detail or change a dialogue as I read between the silences of a moment long gone by. Finally, I have a thousand stories of a handful of memories. A thousand ways of feeling you by my side.

I sail in your love
Every new moon to full moon
My timeless journey.

Kiss of Karma

Purba Chakraborty

No one can escape the *kiss of karma*
Honeyed or poisoned
Sweet or bitter;
You reap what you sow
You can call it Newton's third law
Or the divine poetic justice.
What you throw around
Comes back in your bosom.
She can't be manipulated or deceived
She can't be bribed or bought
To Her, your mines of gold are ashes of dust
To Her, a heart of gold is
Worth thousands of rubies and diamonds.

Your Name

Purba Chakraborty

Nailed to your name
Like sun to the sky
Like grass to the earth
Like fire to the candle
Like blood to the heart
Entwined with your existence,
This *Love* feels like *Art*.

About Purba Chakraborty

Purba Chakraborty is an author of 7 books. She has written 3 novels (Canvas of a Mind, The Hidden Letters, Walking in the streets of Love and Destiny), 1 novella (You Came like Autumn) and 3 poetry books (Mythological Monologues, Letters from the Soul, The Heart Listens to No One).

She is the founder and CEO of Learning Literature with Purba. She is the editor-in-chief of The LLP Magazine. She is an educator, YouTuber, Podcaster, blogger, and a content writer. She is the co-compiler and co-editor of 'The Language of Love' and 'The Language of Divinity' poetry books.

Inner child caring for homely love

Abhirami A.R.

The inner child within us craves love,
Whether from home or another circle.
No matter if we are infants, children or adults
At times, we must face sorrow,
Even in the comfort zones we cherish most.

In the midst of it all, we long for love –
A love wrapped in understanding.
Understanding shares a bond with love,
A bond so true that all can relate to it.

We all crave the warmth of home,
For home is our ultimate sanctuary
In sorrow, we seek its love the most.

May the Almighty bless those
Who are drowning in the sea of sorrow.

About Abhirami A.R.

Abhirami A.R. is a post graduate in English
literature and a B.Ed. student at Sree Narayana
Guru Kripa College with English as her optional
subject. She is passionate about teaching, research

and writing. She aspires to become an assistant professor. She enjoys exploring psychoanalysis, feminism, and literature while engaging in academic discussions and creative pursuits.

Okay or Not Okay? (A poetry on marital rape)

Aditi Sharma

They called me princess and Indeed I was
I blame them for neglecting all my flaws.
Wrapped in love part of their heart
Like a puzzle that would never depart.
A silk blouse and nicely fitted skirt
Going to her future that she thought no one would divert
Twenty-three whose wings never were restricted
Entered in office and her personality all strongly depicted
Met a guy who helped her in the work
Fell in love with him and with his every quirk
A puzzle whose piece was meeting another piece.
It's love. It's fate...never thought it would make her cease.
She expected divinity; tender love from him
The night I married my heart was at the brim
Kisses were smooth hugs were boundless
His love for her...she felt was countless
Days rolled by...love was compromised by daily chores
My decisions My body wasn't mine but now more yours
I and you were not we any more...identities were distinct

Intimacy, sex, romance were not an affection but
more a conflict
Bruises at my body they say are a sign of passion
My heart aches why he doesn't understand this
compassion
Wakes up in the morning I suddenly see he is not
here
Maybe he has gone leaving me in this indifferent air
I am not well today next night I said
He gave me a glass of water and a pill and put me
on that bed
He was on me I could see the aggression on his face
Soon he got up wore the clothes as if he was the
ultimate ace
My eyes were wide open and I was all numb
But suddenly I remember I have to make food for
some
I was slightly back to life when he was away
My children were too small to understand that this
smile was just halfway
Next day I prayed to God like an innocent child
That please make today's night a bit mild
He came home I served the meal
Switched the television on and said what's this
nonsense appeal
I read the words silently repetitively and my heart
skipped a beat
It was something like section 375 marital rape
My hands stopped while serving *chapattis* and I
gazed at the television like I was a magnetic tape
Then they said it's not a crime if you are married by
religious institutions

And my husband smirked a bit and said I knew
these ladies have a habit of making unnecessary
revolutions
Soon I got to bed which I felt was like a cemetery
This time his aggression was doubled maybe after
hearing the news that this is not cautionary
I am bound with the chains of silence throughout
my life
Because I want to be labelled as a good and an
appealing wife
I tried to escape like a creature crawling from the
suffocating four walls
But how can I forget that you all taught me...*Oh
marriage is above all! Oh marriage is above all!*

About Aditi Sharma

Aditi Sharma is a fearless poet and scholar,
wielding language as a weapon against silence. Her
revolutionary verses dismantle oppressive
narratives, with a searing poem on marital rape
igniting echoes that challenge norms. On the path to
pursue a PhD in English literature, she fuses
academia and activism to reshape the boundaries of
power and voice.

Grammar of Loss

Aishwarya Vedula

I write you into being,
shape you from syntax and soft syllables,
a sonnet with no volta,
a stanza I can't escape.
You exist in the subjunctive—
if only, should have, might still—
a clause without a consequence,
a sentence that never arrives.

I conjugate our undoing
in irregular verbs:
to love, to leave, to lose—
all the same in second-person past.
Your silence, a punctuation mark
I never learned to place.
An ellipsis when I needed closure,
a question mark curled like a doubt.

I hold onto our vowels—
open, unguarded, round-mouthed oaths
that never quite closed.
But your consonants remain sharp,
cutting where I didn't expect a stop.
I shift into metaphor,
because direct address is too brutal—
you, a semicolon between what was

and what wasn't enough.

Red ink runs through my revisions,
but every attempt to erase you
is met with the permanence of print—
a love letter turned erratum.

Each time I try to unwrite you,
the margin widens,
the page fills itself again.
I tell myself language is my power,
but what use is poetry
when the grammar of loss
is the only thing left to speak?

About Aishwarya Vedula

Aishwarya Vedula is a literature major, poet, and visual artist from India. She has published three chapbooks and frequently contributes to literary journals. She is currently working as an English lecturer and plans to pursue a PhD in Film Studies. She believes artistic freedom is essential to truly experiencing life.

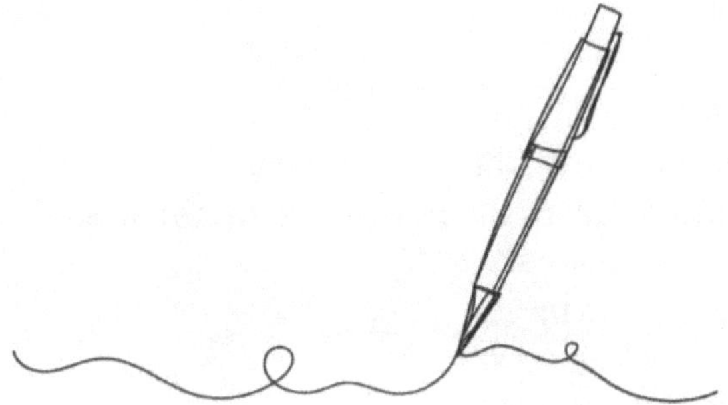

Sempiternal

Ananya Chaudhuri

Soothing whispers of yesteryear
Assimilate with the new found aesthetics.
They amalgamate
They intertwine
They coalesce
With one another.
Avant-garde and bourgeoisie kiss
Stories are woven
Memories are made
Warmth is cherished
With their heart and soul
In one place we all call "home".

About Ananya Chaudhuri

Ananya Chaudhuri (B.A, M.A, B.ed in English)
finds writing poetry cathartic which she began at the
age of nineteen. She embraces life with enthusiasm
and optimism which gets reflected in her poems.

An Unremarkable Life

Anushka Mitra

(1)

Diya was going through her important files on a rainy evening. A melodious playlist was being played on her phone. She made it with her best friend's favourite songs. She smiled every time Mukti's favourite part of the songs came up. She shut the file at hand and leaned back against a pillow. The world looked small through her 18th-floor window. With the pitter-patter, Diya's mind travelled back in time.

It was pouring down. Ten-year-old Diya was standing under the shade of a closed shop, looking up with an overcast face. She had worn her new white shoes. She watched one of her classmates go home, happy and uncaring about her dirty white shoes.

(2)

Diya sat beside that classmate the next day. She was nervous in a new school. The classmate greeted her.

"I am Mukti. What is your name?"

"Diya."

"Nice to meet you, Diya." She had smiled. Diya too.

Since then, they remained inseparable throughout school. Diya often wondered how and why Mukti never left her. Because with time Diya developed an aversion towards the world. She hardly understood why but she couldn't see any purpose of living. On the other hand, Mukti bubbled with life. She saw light even when there was not any.

It was in 10th-grade when Diya first attempted taking her own life. Her puppy "Coco" had died due to a virus attack. She tried everything to save that little life but failed. The sudden loss and empty room towered over Diya. Her heart felt emptier yet heavy. She slit her wrist.
When she opened her eyes in the hospital, her parents hugged her. When she came back, Mukti was there with a cooing puppy and a smile. They called the little happiness Lilly. Coco's loss was never erased. But the presence of Lilly gave Diya a hope to live.

(3)

"Hey listen. How about we live together in an apartment and don't give a fuck about boys?" The 12th-grade board exams were around the corner. They were studying together one evening.

"But you want to fuck boys." Diya smirked. Mukti grinned.

"You too don't seem to be disinterested." Mukti wiggled her eyebrows, "Ok we can date or hook-up but we stay together because why not? See we are so coordinated – you cook, I clean. We'll make a more perfectly harmonious living than any actual couple."

Diya laughed seeing Mukti's proud face after pitching her idea on "How to Crack Life? – Move In with Bff."

They were so happy that monsoon. After exams both stayed together, went to shopping, cooked, and ate together, did movie nights, danced together, braided each other's hair, and experimented make-up. Mukti turned out to be horrible at that.

Diya chuckled looking at the photo frame on her table. Mukti's face looked perfect while Diya's was giving a tough competition to ghosts. White powder, blotches of blush, and to say the eyeliner was uneven would be an understatement. Beginning from the inner corners of her eyes, the shivering liner reached her temples. Mukti's father loved both artists so he had to capture their arts.

That winter was blue. Diya attempted to end her life again. Mukti came to hug her while Diya bawled her eyes out. Her father died.

"You can't run away like this always. Promise me you won't ever do something so rash like this." Mukti spoke vehemently. Diya nodded.

(4)

Their college years were eventful, busy, accomplishing, and successful. They could not be physically together as planned. They went to different universities. But they met every once in a while, talked over calls, and kept each other updated through texts. Diya even stopped going to therapy. The universe conspired for the duo to stay together. They got jobs in the same city. They moved in.

The day they moved in together, their happiness knew no bounds. From *Chaats* to dessert, beers and movies for the first half of the night. Their ecstasy took things a notch further. They cooked a plan to have husbands one day only to have them also move in there. Then their conversation turned juicy for the rest of the night. Mukti confessed to have met someone special in life, Raghav. When he video called, Diya and he immediately bonded over Mukti's horrible choices in men prior Raghav.

Life rolled on its own. The girls' nights were mostly busy—sometimes dull, sometimes lively, sometimes gloomy, sometimes upsetting, sometimes happy drunk, sometimes sad drunk, sometimes fun. The girls were indeed harmonious or were they forcing themselves to be?

Slowly Diya found herself slipping into the darkest abyss of her mind again. She did not realise it entirely until she caught a sleepy Mukti picking up the bottle to drink water. The bottle that contained poison and a day-long contemplation of death.

"Here, drink from glass." Cold sweating Diya offered a safe glass of water to Mukti under the dim light.

"What's the difference anyway? Anyway thanks." Mukti's sleep laced complaint and half-closed eyes caused a surge of relief in Diya's heart. She saw the horror, the price of self-induced death that night. She could not afford it.

Diya kissed Mukti's forehead hugging her. Mukti was too sleepy to detect the tremor in her best friend's body. Once Mukti fell into a deep slumber, Diya flushed the water and burnt the bottle. Sleep did not visit her the entire night. She realised that she was harmful to the person who loved her like a sister. All her life, Mukti had been nothing but patient with her. Unfortunately, she was nothing but a threat, a danger to her dearest friend. She thought. So, Diya returned to her hometown to live with her mother. The sudden decision surprised and equally hurt Mukti. But Diya said, "I have to look after Maa. She's alone."

Diya's mother embraced her daughter protectively when she arrived at her doorstep. She was happy that her daughter chose to live this time, she chose to revisit her therapist and stay alive, live life.

(5)

Many years passed ever since. Diya felt her gloomy past was so far yet so close. She was content with her little family of three; her husband, a little daughter, and herself. Her mother left her long ago. But this time grief did not come with the urge to cut her wrist. She hoped her mother felt proud from heaven. Diya found Mukti right beside her as she navigated herself through the responsibilities of a daughter and pain of becoming an orphan. Mukti was present as the guardian when she got married. It was a small wedding but merriment touched the skies. Mukti flew in within twenty-four hours of Diya giving birth, to be right beside her best friend. Mukti's beaming face after holding her niece for the first time had brought tears to Diya's eyes.

Even after so many years, nothing had changed between them. Mukti was all Diya had as her extended family. When Diya was learning to live her life, Mukti provided her with the extra support whenever she needed. Unfortunately, the memories of herself being there for Mukti had faded alongside many others in which Diya felt peaceful. Was it because of all the medications? Was it a trick of her wicked brain or God's way of punishing her? Or was it because indeed she was insufficient as a friend? How could she vividly remember only the days where the dusks were sombre and night were unending?

"Hey witch! I am coming on the 20th with Raghav. The adoption procedures have been finalised too. We are permanently shifting. And now we will be officially neighbours!!!! Our kids will grow as siblings like us!!!"

Peace. Diya felt it reading the text from Mukti again and again. Even though, she felt that the story of her life was not remarkable. If anything, she felt like an ungrateful selfish person who was given more than they deserved. She was glad she decided to live to honour those blessings.

About Anushka Mitra

Anushka Mitra, Kolkata-based English Literature postgraduate, explores human psychology and Feminism in her writing. Her creative writing appears in *Otherwise Engaged* (2024), *Creative Flight Journal* (2024), and *Powerless* (2025) by CultureCult Press. She has also authored academic articles published in *Critical Gender Studies Journal* (2024) and *Creative Flight Journal* (2024).

The Wrong Way

Avishi

Hold my hand but don't pull me close,
If that happened we will become a ghost.
My touch in your life will shed petals of your roses
And in the hour of your darkest night
Maybe you'd be left with thorns, leaves, letters,
poems, proses with so many dried dead roses.
Don't look into my eyes,
That moment may turn into a curse,
I may ruin your whole world,
With my own problems.
So, love me but stay away.
Make me feel wanted but never touch me that way.
Hold my heart but never bare handed
And I will hold yours with the softest of the touch.
Like butterfly wings I will love you so much
But I will let you go if my bucket gets filled,
If it reaches above my head,
I will let you go,
'Cause I wouldn't want you to suffer something that
isn't yours!
So, hold my hand tight when it all feels blue
But when all of my parts get cut, leave it and run
away.
What if the knife touches you?
Why would I want to hurt you?

About Avishi

Avishi is just another soul trying to figure out why she has been on this planet for 17 years now. You can mail her your reviews at <u>oywavishi@gmail.com</u> and insta- @oywavishi.

Grief eats me alive

Ayush Adhikary

Grief eats me alive
It follows me everywhere
Making it difficult for me to thrive,
As life becomes a living nightmare.

Does it always accompany regret?
I ask myself as I process this loss
My heart never seems to forget,
While I learn embracing this chaos.

They say grief is love unexpressed
Then why does it feel traumatizing?
For love was an exuberant grand fest,
While I sit here with my heart incising.

Maybe grief makes you wise
For it accustoms you to solitude
I hope you see tomorrow's sunrise,
With love, light and gratitude.

<u>About Ayush Adhikary</u>

Ayush Adhikary is a 23-year-old aspiring
filmmaker from Mumbai. He loves reading and

writing poetry, photography, singing, playing the guitar, watching theatre and movies (obviously) when he is not working as an assistant director on sets.

Those Hands

Ayushi Mishra

Those hands that guided me to walk,
Those hands that took me to school for the first
time,
Those hands that used to cut the cake on my
birthday,
Those hands that taught me to burst crackers,
Those hands that mastered me to ride a bicycle,
Suddenly jerked to complete the lifecycle.

My heart is aching, brain is shattered,
Ears are restless to hear his chatter.
Eyes are longing to have his vision,
Nothing can be done but the quick revision.

The harassing mind knows the loss is beyond repair,
Nevertheless, brings futility and despair.
Mind is still wandering between dream and reality,
No part of me is able to accept this brutality.
Death is the dish which no one wants to taste,
But will be served to everyone's plate.

In the gloomy dismal way,
Nothing but the belief in God stays.
He is the one who will pave the way,
Calm the mind and restrict to astray.

About Ayushi Mishra

Ayushi Mishra, born on May 21,1999, in Patna, Bihar, is a student of English literature with a Master's degree from Central University of South Bihar. Her academic interests include Gender Studies and Film Studies, with experience in writing a Master's level dissertation. Beyond academia, Ayushi enjoys reading novels, composing poetry and music. She is currently pursuing a degree in Hindustani classical music.

The Girl in the Mirror

Camellia Shha

I look at myself in the mirror and find a familiar girl
staring back at me.
She resembles me.
Her eyes... they're just like mine,
But as far as I remember, they used to shine.
She smiles, but her smile doesn't reach her eyes.
She lost herself trying to be validated,
And you ask—what was the price?

The place she's in is an abyss,
Full of stories she dares not reminisce.
Her confidence was trampled on, like grass weighed
down by morning dew.
Here, humans are few.
Hahaha... her accent is funny and braggy,
The way she pronounces things is so crappy.
Oh! So, she's from the city,
She must be so witty.

Her nose is crooked,
And hence, she checks herself at every nook.
Her face looks pale;
Now, all she wants is to hide under the veil.
She wears specs,
Needing better vision perhaps.

Again, I find that girl looking at my soul through
that piece of designer glass.
I can't help but wonder what's left of her past.
Will she fight to unravel those shackles
And win the unspoken battles,
Or forever be chained by the judgments?

I believe she'll overcome all the hurdles and lie,
Because one cannot control the vastness of an
ocean, no matter how much and what they try.

While I turned my back to the mirror ready to leave,
SHE – THE GIRL IN THE MIRROR asked me
"Who's stronger than the woman who has plucked
all the pieces of her shattered soul?"

About Camellia Shha

Camellia Shha is a poet who scribbles thoughts
whenever inspiration strikes—usually at the most
inconvenient times. With a flair for turning
everyday chaos into verse, she writes about the
messy bits of life, romance, and self-reflection,
while often wondering if plants make better
listeners than people (she's a horticulturist by
profession).

The Night the Moon Shattered: A Dream Fragment

Chinmayi Sharma

It struck me mid-breath,
a sound vast enough to hollow the chest and turn
my gaze skyward—
to beheld the sky's betrayal.
The moon ruptured, fracturing like brittle glass
beneath the hand of a cruel god,
cracks webbed across her face, craters splitting
wide,
from its wounds drifting shards of argent light,
bleeding silken ribbons of silver into the dark sky,
the quiet pale corpse of the lunar orb remembering
it was once stone.

I stood barefoot on the terrace, high above the
writhing streets—
a chorus of footsteps, a wailing multitude bereft of
reason,
faces upturned, then lost again.
The earth convulsed with the screams, a thousand
souls recalling their mortality.
Mothers shrieked—their voices hoarse, raw with
dread,
clutching small sobbing bodies as if flesh alone
could barter against the sky's undoing.

Fear gripped my chest with its iron hands
tightening, muscles coiled, breath shallow,
the ground heaving beneath my feet, begging me to
join the egression of the damned.
But something strange pressed down upon me, a
gravity not born of earth—
I stood rooted, unbreathing,
every instinct to flee swallowed by the ruinous
beauty unfolding above me.

In an instant, fear drowned, sounds withered.
The moon loomed impossibly near—monstrous yet
sublime,
so near I could taste the iron of its death, feel the
sky's cold carcass grazing my lips—
the final, ashen kiss of the soft moon beams.
My hand rose to touch the looming orb, in hopes to
trace the crevices with my mortal skin.
In my eyes bloomed the ruin of it, silver bled over
my skin, a pale coronation,
I stood crowned in the moon's last gleaming.
It stood suspended in the firmament like the
shattered diadem of a celestial king—
too proud to crumble, too broken to reign—
with its each silver remnant a hymn to oblivion.

I saw not decay but a terrible grace—
in the glistening mosaic of ruin, a beauty wrought
from cataclysm.
I felt not fear but the quiet recognition of the
inevitable—death robed in silken gold.
I stood unflinching as the golden veil, thin as a
breath, heavy as eternity,

descended upon me, settled on my skin—an embrace of a warmth long awaited.

About Chinmayi Sharma

Chinmayi Sharma is a 23 years old girl. She has done Masters in English Literature along with NET. The poem that she has written is entitled 'The Night the Moon Shattered: A Dream Fragment'. Like the name suggests, she had an extremely vivid dream about the moon breaking and she as a witness to this apocalypse. She wanted to pen down the imagery of her dream into something concrete.

When May Came

Christina Dcosta

April wept with trembling hands,
her sorrow spilled across the lands.
She cried for love that slipped away,
for words she lost but meant to say.

Then May arrived, so soft, so still,
she didn't force a broken will.
She simply sat and held the space,
a quiet warmth, a slow embrace.

She knelt beside the weary ground
and whispered, *"Bloom, you're safe and sound."*
The tulips stirred, unsure, afraid,
yet reached for light through cracks of shade.

Like hearts once hurt, now torn between
the fear of love and what it means.
The lilacs swayed, their fragrance light,
a fleeting ghost of past delight.

And oh, the roses, scarred yet bold,
still standing tall though storms took hold.
They knew of loss, they knew of pain,
yet still, they turned to hope again.

Perhaps that's all that May can do—

not mend the past or change what's true,
but hold the hurt and make some space
for something new to take its place.

About Christina Dcosta

Christina Dcosta is from Mumbai, currently pursuing her Bachelor's Degree in English Literature. For the past four years, poetry has been her way of capturing emotions, everyday moments, and the beauty of resilience. Her work often explores themes of nostalgia, love, loss, and personal growth, aiming to connect with readers who find comfort in words. Beyond poetry, she is actively involved in literature and community-driven projects, seeking to create spaces where creativity and expression flourish.

Embrace the Emotion

Debashrita Roy Chowdhury

Don't know what is there in mind.
Surrounded with feelings of what kind?
Neither able to disclose nor hide
Keeping it in the corner of heart's side.

Looking at stars at night
Flowing in the silver light
Moon is giving its glance from high
From my heart coming a deep sigh.

When the eyes meet in its pace
The sight always gave an embrace
Words never utter to explain
Feelings were hidden in vain.

When the cool breeze passes
A shivering jerk adores and lushes
Silently with smile and eyes close
Emotions from the heart arose.

About Debashrita Roy Chowdhury

Debashrita Roy Chowdhury is currently residing at
Mandi, Himachal Pradesh. She is

working as a teacher at Oakwood School. From the
school days, her hobby was writing
poems, which turned into her passion in future.
Poetry is where her thoughts meet her soul
and brings out the creativity.

If I were a boy

Dhritika Deka

If I were a boy, I would wake up late;
No one would scold me for skipping the daily
chores.
If I were a boy, I would party late at night
And come back home whenever I pleased,
The neighbours wouldn't judge my character.
If I were a boy, the torment might have been less;
People might have shown sympathy for my pain.
If I were a boy, I could flirt with thousands
playfully,
And no one would disgrace me much.
Instead, my mates would regard me as charismatic
and humorous.
If I were a boy, no one would distance themselves
from me for expressing anger,
it's normalized for them.
If I were a boy, I could roam freely;
Society would forgive my missteps
Without much sharp judgments or strong reactions.
If I were a boy, they wouldn't push me into
marriage before my thirties,
People wouldn't blame me much for not having
kids,
A few years into marriage.
They wouldn't label me infertile or call me
incapable to my face,

Uninvite me from special occasions
Or consider me as the main reason for a divorce.
If I were a boy, I could have helped in emergencies
more freely,
By driving late at night for my loved ones.
I'd receive a bike as my 18th birthday gift -
And the freedom to ride with anyone, anywhere,
anytime wherever feels right.

About Dhritika Deka

During her free hours, Dhritika Deka enjoys immersing herself in crafting down her ideas into poetry, short stories or paragraphs on society or life in general.

August

Diya Gupta

August is decay
She abandons the most beautiful parts of herself
To preserve a sense of her being
She prepares for a season of grief and freezing
Yet hopes for a blooming spring

August is unending rain
She lets it drop from the skies and from the eyes
She can be so heavy; it blurs everything you love
Sometimes she's just a drizzle, a reminder of the
clouds above
But she is always here

August is comfort
She holds you in her embrace until your sunken
soul is healed
She sings to you until you crave every single day
for her melody
She looks at you until you can look yourself in the
eye
She bakes for you until you long for her cookies at
3 in the night

August is home
She is the warmth of my mother's smiles
She is the calm of my father's advice
She is the hope in my brother's eyes

But August is also going away from home
And so, August is on her own

August is alone
She doesn't embody the hot summer spirit
She isn't icy cold like the winter breeze
She is warm and cold and both together but not
enough
She is terrified of the in-betweens
She is the picture of resilience, but also of falling
apart
She celebrates the new dawn but mourns for the
ending, scarred

And like the muddled anatomy of this poem, august
is...confused
She is hurt and she is healing
She is warm and she is frigid
She is absence and she is company
She is forever and she is nothing

I am August
August is me

About Diya Gupta

Diya Gupta is a budding poet from Pune. She is a
psychology student, seeking to explore emotions,
healing and individualism through her writing. She
enjoys getting a peek into the idiosyncrasies of
human beings through art. She loves traveling and

finding herself amidst nature. Her inclination towards literature since childhood moved her to explore writing as a mode of self-expression.

The Invisible Threads

Djeyavartiny Jayakumar

I was unsure what to do,
A stranger's face, an unknown destiny.
Fear and doubt crept in.
Fifty years together, a daunting test.
Would our love grow or would it decline?
Would I be happy or forever in pain?
What if our worlds didn't align?
The decision weighed heavy, night and day.
Questions swirled, like autumn leaves.
Fear whispered, "Is he the one?"

Days passed, and invisible threads wove a tapestry
of fate.
Everyone's approval was a reassuring thread.
The process was moving fast.
Again, fear and doubt crept in.
Questions swirled, like autumn leaves.
Fear whispered again, "Is he the one?"

On a scarlet sunset,
I made the first move, a courageous call in secret.
He might have been surprised, but I was nervous.
I apologized and thanked him, unsure what to do.
The process was moving fast; I needed to know.
"Are you a gentleman?" I asked, standing tall.
A brief silence.

He smiled and said, "Yes, I am," with a gentle tone.
And promised, "I will be forever."

Day by Day,
Hope began to shine,
Trust blossomed, like a rose in bloom.
The universe smiled; our love began.
Our love unfolded, like a work of art.
My heart whispered, "Yes, he is the one"

About Djeyavartiny Jayakumar

Djeyavartiny Jayakumar has completed her masters
in English literature. She is from
Karaikal, Pondicherry. Her above poem is based on
the complexity and beauty of human experience
when it comes to arranged marriage. Some of her
works are "The reflection of full moon in the
mirror", "My only hope", "The scar" titled poem in
the anthology "The language of love" and in Tamil
"Vithiyin kadhalan"

Echo

Elizabeth S George

The buzzing crowd care not to reply
The fluttering leaves dare not to say goodbye
The road lay flat and infinite
While my heart stutters for a single breath

The nights spent in jovial company
And days skipping by like a hummed melody
Yet I remain in this widening chasm
Praying not to be unravelled by anybody

Hello...hello...
Who's there...there ...
Voices, anxiety grow
While alas! It is only my echo

Questions crowd up, clouding the clay
Uncertainties, fears crouching to prey
The past care not to say goodbye
The future dare not reply...

<u>About Elizabeth S George</u>

Elizabeth S George, a literature enthusiast from Adoor, is pursuing her Master's in English Language and Literature at Fatima Mata National College, Kollam. Passionate about art and storytelling, she finds beauty in words, melodies, and the world around her, weaving them into a tapestry of creativity and expression.

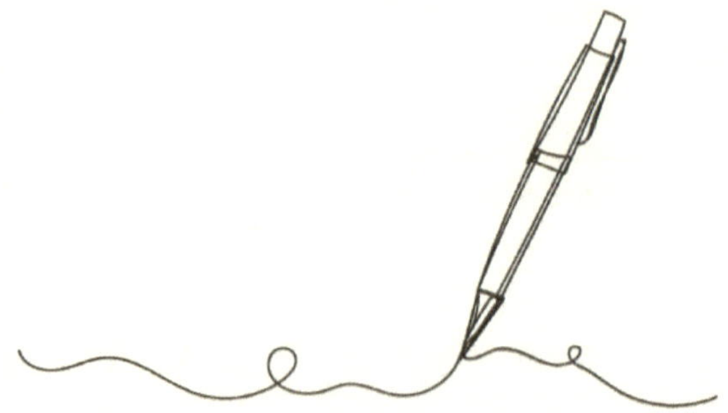

Skin & Bones

Gitika Mittal

I feel unsettled
I think my skin is not mine
a borrowed suit of flesh
I exist in the shadows
visible but never seen
I do not believe that I was meant to be born
a mistake, perhaps my own?
a wandering soul, no light in sight
no destination, no right

I wonder sometimes
what it would be like to die
and then I realise
aren't I already dead?
for my heart may be beating, my lungs still
breathing
but the soul has no light
an empty soul and a broken heart
a passing moment
no end to follow

About Gitika Mittal

Gitika Mittal is a psychology and media student who loves exploring the human mind and how media affects us. She enjoys keeping up with pop culture (read obsessing over), and connecting with others. As an avid reader and a huge K-pop fan, she enjoys learning new things. She writes poetry to capture unspoken thoughts.

Only Yours: A Timeless Bond of Love

Gopika M

I lost myself in your light,
I see myself in you, so bright.
You lighten my world and brighten me,
With your love, patience, and care, you set me free.

Sighing under moonlit skies,
I breathe in the air that you provide.
The fragrance you spread over me,
Is a treasure I hold, just for you and me.

The world calls upon us to the heavens above,
There, we'll spread the beauty of our endless love.
Spending time together, our bond will grow strong,
Forever and always, our love will shine and never
go wrong.

You are my ears, my eyes, my taste,
Through you, I build my future and create.
I see myself through you and you through me,
You are my future, past, and present, my destiny.

About Gopika M

Gopika M is an aspiring writer with a deep love for storytelling and poetry. She is a graduate in English Literature and currently pursuing a B.Ed. in English. She finds inspiration in the beauty of language and its power to evoke emotions. Writing, for her, is a way to capture fleeting moments and unspoken feelings, transforming them into words that resonate with others. Through her poetry, she hopes to create connections, spark emotions, and leave a lasting impression on those who read her work.

From Home to Varanasi

Gunjan Chauhan

Vriti's laughter was a melody, the kind that filled rooms and lingered long after she left. In her small, rustic village, she was the life of every gathering— the one whose joy seemed to defy the constraints of the world. Days were simple but vibrant, filled with games of cards with her paternal uncle and endless chatter with friends. She never wondered about life beyond her village. Why would she? Her world, slow and serene, was enough. But life has a way of challenging our contentment.

One evening, as the sky turned amber, Vriti's elder brother sat her down. "You need to move to Delhi," he announced, his tone final.

Vriti blinked, startled. "Delhi? Why? I'm happy here."

Her brother's gaze softened, but his words were firm. "You have potential, Vriti. You deserve more than this village can offer. You need to study further."

"But—"

"It's decided," he interrupted. "You'll leave next week."

Days later, with her mother by her side, Vriti arrived in Delhi. The city was everything her village wasn't—loud, chaotic, and relentless.

Her first day at school was a nightmare. The classrooms buzzed with confident voices, the students polished and poised. Vriti, with her simple clothes and village accent, stood out like a sore thumb.

"Hey, do they even have schools where you're from?" a girl snickered as Vriti introduced herself.

Another chimed in, "Maybe she's here to teach us how to milk cows."

The room erupted in laughter.

Vriti's cheeks burned, but she held her head high. That night, as she lay on her narrow bed, she whispered to herself, "I'll show them. I belong here."

Weeks turned into months, and Vriti channelled her hurt into her studies. Slowly, her hard work began to speak louder than her accent. Teachers praised her and classmates started seeking her notes. The laughter that once stung her now faded into the background.

Then, in 2018, her world came crashing down.

It was a harmless conversation with a boy—a few exchanged words. But in her family's eyes, it was unforgivable. The news travelled fast, and by the time Vriti returned home during a break, she was greeted with cold stares.

Her uncle, who once played cards with her every evening, refused to meet her eyes. At dinner, his silence was deafening.

"*Bade Papa*," she said softly, her voice trembling, "Will you not talk to me?"

Her sister replied before he could. "No. You've embarrassed all of us."

Vriti's heart shattered. She turned to her uncle, searching for even a flicker of forgiveness. He turned away.

The weight of her family's judgment crushed her. Her grades plummeted, and her dreams of a bright future dimmed. When her 12th-grade results arrived, they were a disappointment. Her family seized the opportunity to pull her back.

"No more college," her father declared. "We trusted you, and look what you've done."

"But *Baba*—"

"No!" he roared. "You'll stay here. We can't risk you losing your way again."

It was her brother who stepped in. "She deserves another chance," he argued. "Let her study in Agra. I'll take responsibility."

Reluctantly, the family agreed.

In Agra, Vriti found a temporary reprieve. She made friends who laughed with her instead of at her. Together, they dreamed of brighter futures. But friendships, she learned, are fragile. By the end of her college years, those who had once been her closest companions had drifted away.

On her final day, she stood alone on the bustling campus. Her best friend walked past her without a word, as if the years they had spent together meant nothing.

"People leave," Vriti murmured to herself, swallowing the lump in her throat. "That's just how it is."

She took a selfie, capturing her solitude. But later, when she searched for the photo, it was gone. She smiled wryly. "Maybe even God didn't want me to carry this."

Her journey took her to Varanasi, a city she had only heard of in passing. For the first time, Vriti lived alone. The girl who once struggled to fold her clothes now managed an entire life. The ghats of the Ganga became her sanctuary. She spent hours by the river, watching its endless flow and finding solace in its quiet wisdom.

One afternoon, as she sat at Manikarnika Ghat, watching the funeral pyres burn, she felt a strange sense of clarity.

"This is where it all ends," she thought, watching the flames rise. "Wealth, beauty, pride—none of it matters. Only kindness does."

The city transformed her. She wandered through its narrow lanes, visited temples alone, and sipped chai at roadside stalls. Strangers shared their stories with her, their words more genuine than the empty promises of the friends she had once trusted.

One evening, she struck up a conversation with an elderly chai vendor.

"You're not from here," he observed, handing her a steaming cup.

"No," she said, smiling. "But this city feels like home."

He chuckled. "That's Varanasi for you. It shows you who you are."

Vriti nodded, her heart full.

Varanasi taught her to embrace change and find strength in solitude. The girl who once feared loneliness now cherished it.

On her last evening in the city, Vriti stood by the Ganga as the sun dipped below the horizon, casting the river in golden hues. In her hand, she held a small *diya.* She knelt by the water's edge, her voice barely a whisper.

"Let this *diya* take my fears, my regrets, and everything I no longer need to carry," she said, releasing it onto the water.

As the *diya* flickered on the surface of the Ganga, Vriti stood still, watching it drift away. The river, in its eternal flow, seemed to carry not just the small flame, but the weight of her past— her struggles, her doubts, her regrets. The water glistened, reflecting the first stars of the evening, and she felt a quiet peace settle over her.

The Ganga had whispered to her that night, and the message was clear: life would always move forward. Just like the river, she too had to continue her journey—letting go of the old; embracing the new.

Vriti looked at the river one last time, then at the dark sky. "I've arrived," she whispered, as though the words were a prayer, a promise to herself.

The city of Varanasi, with its ancient wisdom, had healed the fractures of her heart. It had shown her that in the end, the most important relationship was the one she had with herself. She no longer needed the approval of others to know her worth. She had discovered it for herself.

As she walked away from the Ganga, she felt the weight in her chest lift. She could hear the soft rhythm of the river behind her, but it no longer beckoned her to return. Varanasi had given her what she needed—a sense of belonging that wasn't tied to a place or a person but to her own soul.

With each step, Vriti felt lighter, freer. She smiled, knowing that wherever life took her next, she was ready. Not because she had all the answers, but because she had learned to embrace the unknown.

Her journey wasn't over—it was just beginning. And this time, she was walking with the strength of a woman who had learned to trust herself.

About Gunjan Chauhan

Gunjan Chauhan belongs to Auraiya, Uttar Pradesh. She is a postgraduate in English Literature from

Banaras Hindu University. She has embarked on her writing journey, with her first poem, 'A Tale of Ancient Love', published in the anthology 'The Language of Divinity', reflecting her passion for timeless storytelling.

My Burning Skies

Jagriti Sen

I am always struck with a wave of awe every time my eyes meet the vast stretch of mountains at a distance away from where we sleep. There is nothing new about this scenery, nothing new about the vast plain, barren and muddy land in front of the mountains, nothing new about those mountains themselves. Their slopes are muddy from the rains, battered by the snow and their rocks eroded by the harsh sun. Yet, at night none of it is noticeable. All that is, is a vast stretch of colossal peaks, beyond which lies freedom.

Freedom has become a concept foreign to me. Freedom has become a concept foreign to the last of my people who are still alive, their eyes dull without a flicker of hope. The lands that belong to us are being walked by foreigners with blue eyes and blonde hair. They walk on these lands like they own them, assert their authority with such an audacity it's almost laughable. They drink water from the streams which belong to us. They eat food harvested by our people. They shed warm blood on the ground belonging to the veins of my people. Freedom has become a concept foreign to my land of Polska.

The little bundle in my lap shivers as wind blows through the tent I had built with scrap clothes. My little brother opens his eyes, and looks at me with big brown eyes withered by the holds of fatigue. I brush his hair out of his face, as he looks outside.

"Shooting star!" His weak voice calls out, little fingers pointing at the sky. The innocence of his words makes me choke. My palms lay flat on his ears, as the "shooting star" falls on a village neighbouring ours.

Our land of Polska has been taken by "outlanders". I have no knowledge of who they are or where they come from, just enough to know they mean nothing but harm and cruelty. Their men have bruised us, battered us and murdered us. Their men have murdered my parents, and thrown their bodies in a pile of their sins like a sack of garbage, with no significance. I barely scraped them, as I ran away with my brother. It has been three days, since we have been hiding. The outlanders will kill everyone.

My people have foolishly given up their lives for this land, thrown their bosoms in front of the foreign guns and were ready to do anything but leave their land.

I refuse to die with my people.

Beyond the mountains is the sea, which if I crossed, will take me to another land. I will escape the torture of these foreigners, take my brother with me and escape to a new land, where freedom shall have me. Of course, the feat itself is no easy, but nothing easy ever comes with the pursuit of freedom. I refuse to burn with the skies of Polska, and become one with the same soil which is stained by the blood of my people and the dirt of the sinners who walk on them.

Heavy boots echo through the woods behind us. I press my hands against my brother's mouth, asking him to stay quiet. Ears perked, I peek outside my tent to see two officers at a distance, talking between themselves. They have guns on them.

I slowly come out of the tent when both the officers turn their backs on me, moving ahead. Trying to stay as quiet as possible, I take my little brother in my arms and slowly come out of the tent. It is difficult, under the dark night when
I can see nothing, but it is not the time to think.

"Hey! Who is there?" An officer turns around, walking straight towards the tent. I hold my breath, gripping my brother tightly.

"This tent looks pretty old and beat up." the second officer, with shaggy brown hair grips a piece of a cloth I had used for the tent. It belonged to my mother. My teeth grits, as he rubs his hands off the dust his fingers collected upon touching it. I lean against the tree I am hiding, holding my brother *really really* close to me.

"Someone was living here, Nez. I do not suppose they are here anymore though." The other laughs a sickening laugh, mimicking a gun to his head with his fingers. My fingers curl into my dirty clothes.

"Well, no point of us patrolling this area then. Let's get back." Both the officers start walking away. I wait for some time, some more just in case. After a good 15 minutes or so had passed, I slowly come out of my hiding. The tent was destroyed. I sit down with my brother in my lap, eyes staring at the sky. Even amidst chaos, Polska decorates her night skies with the prettiest of stars. My eyes trace a few, trying to make a shape out of them.

I feel a tug on my shirt. Looking down, I see my brother pointing to his mouth. His eyes droop with tiredness.

I look around me, trying to find something to eat. In the darkness, nothing comes into my vision. There has to be something nearby, after all this area was inhabited by villagers before everything was annihilated. I extend my arm out, trying to feel the dirt for something, and silently praying my brother does not have to sleep hungry another day.

God has an ear after all. My eyes light up as I feel the distinct shape of an apple under my fingers. Grasping it, I take a look to make sure it has not gone bad. It already had a bite taken out of it and had gotten yellow, but other than that, looked safe to eat. I hand it to him.

He holds it so softly and carefully like it is going to disappear. He stares at it, eyes twinkling like the stars in the sky, as if his hands have gotten hold of a treasure so valuable. I smile softly watching him nibble on it. Resting my head against a tree, my eyes flutter shut and soon, I am drifting off.

~~

My feet fall softly on the sand, as I hide behind a big jeep. At a distance, there are three officers sitting around a wooden table outside of their cabin, harbouring a warm cup of coffee, sipping from it occasionally. Under the morning light, I can see their uniforms having a symbol, but not enough to make out what it says. Peeking a bit, I listen to their conversation.

"We have managed to infiltrate the entire village. Any remaining survivor has been killed." The posture of the speaker and the way he salutes the one sitting on the chair tells me he is a subordinate. His boss puts the mug down on the table.

"Good. We can leave in two days. What about the Yealer Mountains? Have there been any escape attempts?" My ears perk with interest at the mention of the mountains.

"A few. We have managed to stop them. It was expected. The only escape route is through the mountains, after all." My brother stirs behind me, my fingers gripping him, warning him to be quiet.

"Set a cabin or two up in the plains before the mountains, just in case. I will contact General Darvis and let him know Operation Polska was successful. May God be with you, Corporal."

Shame on them to even think they deserve to say God's name. The Divine is blind to people like these. I do not stay any longer to listen to the conversation. I quietly move back to where I was. I have to carry my escape plan out tonight. There cannot be a delay anymore.

~~

I grow jittery with each passing minute. Waking my brother up, I tie him with a cloth to me, and cover my face. It is exceptionally dark tonight. Good for me. I step out into the plains, slowly. There is wind blowing, and the Yealer mountains are at a distance. I put one foot after the other, eyes cautiously looking at the surroundings, making sure there is no one here to sabotage us. My brother, as if sensing my anxiety, puts his palm next to my shoulder, a tiny attempt to calm me down. I keep walking towards the mountains, their size getting bigger and bigger the closer I get. At a short distance, I see a cabin with fire lit outside. There does not seem to be anyone out. I have to move cautiously and swiftly, without letting them see me.

It was suspiciously easy to get to the foot of the mountains, without alerting anyone. I glance behind me, the cabin several feet away, my heart beating out of my chest. I pray in my head, and just as I am about to turn around, a voice comes out of the cabin.

"Halt!"

I do not think. I start running up the hills, my brother whimpering behind me, and farther away there are boots running towards me. My speed is slower due to my brother being on my back, but despite that, I run and do not look back. Somewhere in the distance I hear a click followed by a bang, and suddenly I am on the muddy ground of the slopes, my ankles are bleeding out.

My brother falls down at a distance. I am in pain and I do not know if I can run, but with a yell I manage to get up. By the time I do though, the officers are already close enough to catch up. I look at my brother, yelling at him to get up. He looks at me, big innocent star like eyes glistening with tears. I do not have enough time to get him up and running. His little arms reach out to me, voice breaking as he asks for me. The officers are close enough to shoot both of us down. My body pauses, as I step back a few inches.

I refuse to die with my people.

I turn around, and start running. I hear my brother's cries get louder when the officers catch up to him and hold him down. I hear him call my name, begging me to come back for him. There is a yell before there is a shot. Then there is silence. My feet start slowing down as they trudge through the mud. I keep walking until I collapse on the mud. In the silence, I look up at the sky.

The stars do not shine tonight.

About Jagriti Sen

Jagriti Sen is an 18-year-old writer based in Kolkata. She has had her story published before, and is a book enthusiast, who likes to write thriller and horror.

The Chimera

Kusha Bhasin

In a world of murmur, friendly and wide,
Daughter of Typhon and Echidna wandered, with
none beside.
A lion's heart, a goat's sharp horns,
A dragon's tail—it fire scorns.

Mankind vanished, the people feared,
No tender voice, no warmth appeared.
The boundless sky had stars shining bright,
But none was there to share the night.

The Chimera looked for one who would see,
Beyond the ogre, a soul so free.
Then, by a lake so still, so blue,
A lonely child sat with eyes so true.

Reached out a hand, so tiny, so kind—
No fear, no doubt, just the pure heart of mankind.
You are so strange, but so am I.
We both strolled; I'm wondering why;

A friendship grew, so strong, so rare—
Two friendless souls who had a lot to share.
And so, they walked, both beast and boy,
A world once deserted was now filled with joy.

About Kusha Bhasin

Kusha is a teacher and poet who finds beauty in everyday life. She writes with an open heart, exploring emotions, nature, and the quiet moments that shape us. She enjoys reading, reflecting, and finding meaning in the little things.

Against all Odds

Linda V

Linda's small, one-room house in the Bombay slums was a world of its own. She lived with her parents, her mother being her closest confidante. The narrow alleys and cramped spaces were a far cry from the ideal childhood, but Linda's spirit remained unbroken.

As she sat on the floor, trying to focus on her studies, the cacophony of children playing and factories humming in the background made it a herculean task. Yet, Linda's determination and innate intelligence propelled her to excel academically. She would often return home with prizes and accolades, beaming with pride.

One day, as she walked in with a trophy, her mother's face lit up. "Linda, honey, you've done it again! I'm so proud of you!"

Linda smiled, hugging her mother tightly. "Thanks, mom. I couldn't have done it without your support."

As days went by, God gifted them a beautiful house in Kerala and they moved into their new home. It was a beautiful farm house in a beautiful area. They were all very happy.

Just when they thought everything was going fine, disaster struck. One fateful day, Linda woke up hearing her mother's cries. Her father suffered a devastating stroke, leaving him paralyzed. The family's world was turned upside down. Linda and her mother both worked tirelessly to make ends meet as well as take care of the father 24/7. Linda, now in her youth, took on the responsibility of caring for her father.

As she sat beside her father's bedside, holding his hand, Linda's mother came in, exhausted.
"Linda dear, how's dad?"

Linda looked up, tears welling up in her eyes. "He's not responding, mom. I'm so scared."

Her mother sat down beside her, wrapping a comforting arm around her shoulders. "We'll get through this, Linda. We have to be strong for dad."

In the midst of chaos, Linda found solace in her faith. She would often pray, seeking guidance and strength. One day, as she sat in the small chapel near her home, she poured her heart out to God.

"Dear God, please help us. We're struggling so much. Give us the strength to carry on."

As she prayed, a sense of peace washed over her. She felt a gentle whisper in her heart, urging her to trust in God's plan.

In 2018, a devastating flood hit Kerala and it swept through their homes, inundating their home. Linda's family was forced to seek shelter elsewhere, leaving behind their belongings. They had to relocate quickly to a safer place. The volunteers took the bedridden dad in a stretcher through the flood waters. Linda's mother clutched her hand. "Linda, darling, we'll get through this. We have each other."

Linda nodded, trying to hold back tears. "I know, mom. We'll start again."

As the days turned into weeks, and the weeks into months, Linda's father's condition worsened. The stroke had left him bedridden, and he was unable to move or speak coherently. But what was even more heart-breaking was that he had lost his mind. He would often lash out at his wife and daughter, the two people who loved him the most.

Linda's mother would try to feed him, bathe him, and care for him, but he would push her away, shouting obscenities and curses. Linda would try to talk to him, to comfort him, but he would turn his face away, his eyes filled with anger and hatred.

Despite his behaviour, Linda and her mother continued to care for him, showering him with love and compassion. They would pray for him, asking God to heal his mind and body, to restore him to his former self.

But as the days went by, Linda's father's behaviour became more and more erratic. He would curse Linda, telling her that she was worthless, that she was the reason for his suffering. Linda would try to ignore his words, to remind herself that he didn't mean what he was saying, that he was just a sick man.

But it was hard. The words cut deep, and Linda would often find herself crying in her room, feeling hurt and rejected. But she would always turn to God, praying for strength and comfort.

"God, please help me," she would pray. "Please give me the strength to care for my father, to love him despite his behaviour. Please heal his mind and body, and restore him to his former self."

And as she prayed, Linda would feel a sense of peace wash over her. She would feel God's presence, His love and comfort surrounding her. And she would know that she was not alone, that God was with her, guiding her and strengthening her.

With renewed strength and courage, Linda would face another day, caring for her father, loving him despite his behaviour, and trusting God to heal and restore him.

Years went by, and Linda grew into a compassionate and wise young woman. She became a teacher, beloved by her students for her kindness, patience, and unwavering commitment to their well-being. As she stood before her classroom, Linda knew that she had found her true calling – to inspire, to educate, and to help her students live a morally good life.

One day, as she was teaching a lesson on perseverance, one of her students asked, "Miss, how do you stay so strong despite all the challenges you've faced?"

Linda smiled, her eyes shining with tears. "It's because I've learned to trust in God's plan. He's always with us, guiding us through the tough times. And I've had my family's love and support throughout."

As she looked out at the sea of young faces before her, Linda knew that she had truly found her purpose – to spread hope, love, and light in a world that often seemed dark and unforgiving.

About Linda V

Linda is an English teacher from Kerala. She loves art and literature. With a passion for art and creativity, she expresses herself through various mediums and shares her talents on Linda's

ArtandCraft Channel on YouTube. She is a firm believer in God who has been her strength throughout. She resides with her husband and parents.

My Quest

Mahi Patel

I got my first wedding proposal at nineteen, is it normal? My parents named me, Padmakshi. The lotus-eyed, associated with Goddess Saraswati. But, did they really want me to be that? My questions and curiosity never end. Especially today, when I heard the conversations between my *maa* and *baba*. They have been stressed about my age and wanted me to get married to an OCI man just so that I have a good life outside India. I have been reflecting upon this idea for the longest, as it has become our daily dinner table conversation that life outside India after marriage gives you security, opportunity and better living than in India.

Although, isn't it obvious that marriage needs to have trust, understanding and love, and this union needs to be selfless? I have observed that for the green card in hand, people marry without even knowing each other. The thirst to be a foreigner and being unconventional in your own marriage sends a chill to me. Nevertheless, this is a sensitive topic with branches of opinions. What matters to me now is to enrol myself into a creative writing program and become a writer, like Virginia Woolf and Jhumpa Lahiri. Yes, you can say I am a feminist with determined heart and resilience.

Today, after waking up, I knew exactly what I wanted: that black *bindi*, *poha* and courage to deny that marriage proposal. At the breakfast table, like always *baba* was reading the newspaper with disgust reflecting with each word he read. I mustered up all my will power and with an innocent face, I confessed my desire to be a writer and not being married. *Baba* just looked me and smiled. That smile was enough to let me know that he was expecting my confession. *Baba* with his heavy voice said, "I was waiting for an answer, and I knew what your heart desired".

Those words are still engraved in my mind, even after so many years.

Today I am twenty-nine, YES, this age doesn't scare me at all. Here, I am unmarried, finding myself and giving a beautiful life to my girl. Yes, she is adopted. It was the most absurd thing I can do with my life, according to my dear relatives as no one would marry me, but why can't an unmarried woman with her daughter get married, the questions come again.

The definitions of marriage, love and most importantly, trust have been very convincingly moulded by society, as being a certain age, height, qualification and OCI. Marriage doesn't demand age, height or OCI. A marriage with love, understanding, and commitment survives happily. And, I have no regrets of the choices I made in my life. It was risky, uncertain and dangerous but I wanted every bit of it. Being a writer, reading and observing human behaviour made me realize we are made of unlimited potential. What makes us stop is our fear of failure followed by shame.

Maa has shown me the true definition of endurance and patience throughout her life. I will tell her story another day, but being married at an early age and sacrificing your needs in order to meet your spouse's needs was normal during her generation which I would never question to, rather I would respect it.

Women in my life have shown me that women can do anything, when they have an understanding man in their life. The role of a man in a woman's life is undeniably the most important one, I have respect for all those men who truly understand what a woman want. I am ready to wait until I meet that man.

My life as a single girl child has been every second of self-exploration and quest for numerous answers. Being called weird and different in academic years to being able to be comfortable in my own skin and needing no company and sitting by myself alone and happy.

I have taken every criticism as a moment of reflection on why I was considered different than others just because I don't have siblings. The need for having company never really affected me as I wanted to be independent as soon as possible to give back to my parents. I was labelled as being confident and unaffected with a stoic personality. But that doesn't mean I don't need a friend, preferring quality over quantity has been my motive.

This is going all over the place, but I know there are many who does resonate with my views.
At this stage of my life, I have realised not all questions that life throws at you needs to have answers. Being your true self is the best answer, as at the end, we would have our share of experience and learning. Life changes, every single minute, it's just that we don't see it. My life changed from the marriage proposal, to adopting my little girl, to my quest coming to rest with belief in surrendering.

Lastly, as Padmakshi, I am just a girl who dream to have a husband, a family of her own, and a girl who finds comfort in silence. A house in mountains, close to nature and its abundance, providing me serenity in my unsettling days of writer's block.

You women have come a long way; a little reminder for all your unsaid needs that you convinced that you didn't deserve. You deserved every bit of it and more. Life is unpredictable and so are we; we make mistakes and learn. For me, what matters is good intention and never listening to societal opinion, as they don't live my life.

Padmakshi, at last became who she really is - lotus eyed, unaffected of the mud around her, blooming with courage, resilience and beauty.

About Mahi Patel

Mahi Patel is a MA English student. Being complimented for her public speaking skills, she wants to spread her words of encouragement through her writing. She has roots from Gujarat. Hyderabad has her heart, and travelling to India made her realise where her soul truly belongs to.

Bare Minimum

Mercy Jones

A little smile is enough to break that silence.
A little time is enough to pull the closeness.
A little warmth is enough to get the wholesome.
A little love is enough to swaddle the tears.
A little care is enough to bundle the joy.
A little effort is enough to grab the attention.
A little loyalty is enough to burn the royalty.
A little excitement is enough to drive far away.
A little sharing is enough to be alluring.
A little laugh is enough to rumple the thoughts.
A little fairness is enough for the bubbling of the
whole Caboodle.
A little of me is enough to melt down.
A mere little is enough for that mere being.
A little of that is becoming little in accepting the
little.

<u>About Mercy Jones</u>

Mercy Jones is a student exploring arts with the
blend of literature and sparks of creativity. Her
work reflects a curious mind, a love for art, and a

deep observation of life's nuances. She believes art has the power to evoke emotions, spark imagination, and create connections, and she strives to bring that essence into every sketch she draws, every word she weaves, and every idea she shapes.

(Art work by Mercy Jones)

Womb

Pankaj Kumar Pati

The host whom I love the most
Abodes in the hut of my heart.
Built with the clay of sheer feeling
Fenced with the joy and wailing.

Her presence is constant, eternal
Like heart's beating and Sun's rising
Her beauty is infinite and ethereal
Like flower of Eden blooming.

Her fragrance, an ever-lasting joy
Her touch, the most soothing feeling ever.
Her jocund company, an undying convoy
Her love, the most invaluable treasure
Her womb, a palatial heavenly abode
She is my mom; she is my God.

About Pankaj Kumar Pati

Pankaj Kumar Pati resides at Joka, Kolkata, West
Bengal. He is currently working as an

Administrative Officer, Bureau of Applied Economics & Statistics, Government of West Bengal. He has an academic background in English Literature. Writing in Bengali & English is his hobby.

A Blessing called Nature

Rahel H Rajan

The ray of sun
Gifts me shine
The touch of breeze
Makes me calm
The twinkle of stars
Gives me smile
The song of bulbul
Taught me music
The loneliness of moon
Showed me solitude
The darkness of night
Grants me myself
The colony of ants
Describes me unity
The waves of sea
Teaches me life
Nature always delivers
Me something
What can I give as
A return gift
Okay, I'll offer
My soul
Again nature
Presents me peace.

About Rahel H Rajan

Rahel H Rajan is a post graduate in English Literature who aspires to be an author one day. Currently she is working as a part time tutor and is also preparing for competitive exams. Her hobbies include reading, listening to music and watching movies. She loves to read thrillers the most and write reviews about books on social media. She is a family girl who values true bonding than virtual show off.

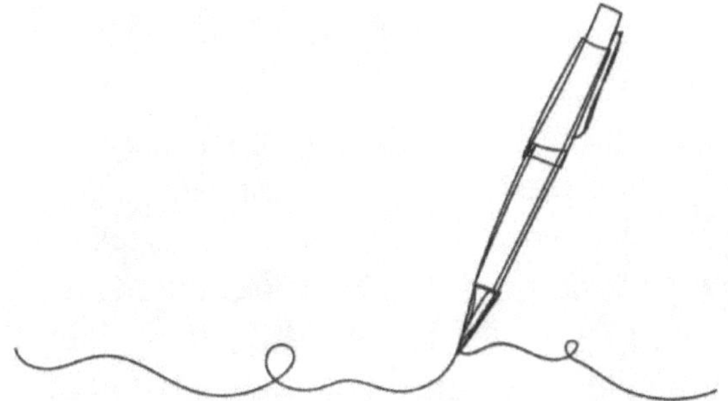

Crossing the River of Faith

Rashmi Kumari

Reached at the bank, flowing in silence
Reconciling the past life, in flashback piece
Rotten by its smelly shelf, piling up kites
Remembering the wounds of fire, quenching in rites
Raven on the other side, waiting after a long mile
"Ride! Ride!", wrecked boat man gave guide
Rugged hands and bristly skin, with old smile in
peace
River dear! Bless the traveller, spoken words of
man
Right behold? Even with the throng hands.
Rather it gave food and shelter to my shady sands
Rest at shelter, and sit away from the selfish world
Replete the barren soul, in the pious water survived
Renunciate raven creating rambunctious on your ray
Radiance and ravishing face recuperating all way
"Have faith! While crossing the river"
"Leading to the world of redemption in eternal
love"

About Rashmi Kumari

Rashmi Kumari is a PhD scholar and a writer by
heart. She believes in spreading love through the

wisdom of words. She lives in the mountains, close to nature and it gives her faith to believe in love and humanity.

The Radcliffe Line

Rashmi Vats

Her red dupatta fell
From her whitening head.
She looked up at the house,
The creases on her forehead
Deepened. Her eyes searching
All over the walls for
A familiar crevice, a known nook.
She lifted her hand
To the doorbell, hesitating.
She stepped back, her curious
Eyes stared at the house, looking
For answers she already knew.
The house stared back,
Hunched in understanding,
Regretful of its newness.
She ran her hands over the door,
No recognition, no recollection.
The house reverberated
From surrogate memories-
Of walls, windows, doors
And the people inside.
The ground shook from
Footsteps stuck in the past,
And the dust of her
Childhood unfurled, stuck on
Her forehead. Outside her, calm
And silence reigned. The sun

Went far back
Into the horizon, and shadows grew
Longer. Her head lifted slowly,
Her eyes unlit and dark
As the sky, fell
On a piece of wood
Stuck above the window-
'Estd. 1979'- a tear rolled down
The crevices of her skin.
Her eyes roved over
The house, over
The Radcliffe Line peeking
From the cracks in the walls.
She flinched, accepted and
Adjusted her red dupatta,
Hiding the white again.

About Rashmi Vats

Rashmi Vats is a freelance editor and writer
currently residing in New Delhi. She
earned her MA in English Literature from Delhi
University. Rashmi enjoys reading
Japanese detective fiction and the poems of Gieve
Patel.

The Farewell Song of the Battlefield's Bloom

Richa Sharma

A form divine, destined flame,
A son of valour, known by name.
On the thirteenth day of war so vast,
He faced the maze; his fate was cast.

Govind knew the coming dread,
A storm would rise, a soul would shed.
A chariot turns towards the night,
Where doon would claim its mortal right.

An epic tale began that day,
As arrows sliced through the skies of grey.
The Kaurava force in their ruthless might,
Broke all their vows to win the fight.

His weapons fell and the shield was torn,
Yet the fire inside was battle-born.
When Karna seized his bow away,
His sword still danced in war's array.

From wounded lips, the words still burned,
Where destiny and courage took a turn.
A battle raged within his soul,
As life and death had lost control.

The roars grew wild, clashes bright,

A warrior fell, yet shone in light.
Yudhishthira scorned the plea of mercy's touch,
For death itself had asked too much.

Duryodhana's mace had struck the ground,
Dust with breath was twined and bound.
Yet far away, in silent grief,
Uttara clung to lost belief.

With blood-stained lips and fearless gaze,
He met his end in the crimson blaze.
He sent his mother's heart a word--
"Though fallen, I have not been stirred."

Karna stood with his fate resigned,
For words had failed his weary mind.
One final wound, one last breath,
Where honour clashed with fated death.

And through the songs of time's embrace,
A legend rose in death's own place.
Though weapons fell in endless tide,
His face still glowed with fearless pride.

Though lost, his tale shall never fade,
A warrior true in fate he stayed.
He marched into the jaws of doom,
Yet carved his name beyond the tomb.

About Richa Sharma

Richa Sharma is a literature enthusiast, researcher, and educator with a strong academic background. Her academic interests span Victorian literature, dystopian fiction, gothic literature, and mythological narratives. Currently preparing for a PhD in English Literature, she aims to contribute meaningful research to contemporary literary studies.

Lost

Ronak Shah

Lost — 'tis the story of everyone
It's the story of life's compromise
When expectations are not fulfilled
When hope dies and romance lies

It's when you feel love in all your soul
In an indifferent and disregarding world
It's when you're ready for the next step
But the path ahead is all circles and twirls

It's when your beating heart aches for more
But your declarations fall on deaf ears
The grinding gears of time forever-shifting
And you try your utmost to hide your tears

It's when your passion rises to fight
Challenging the infinite void of the firmament
Dissipating inevitably, as Natural Order dictates
With an ashen being left behind full of torment

Lost — 'tis indeed the story of everyone
It's the poetry of love's demise
When promises are seldom kept
'Tis but Providence giving you a sobering rise.

Kintsugi

Ronak Shah

A barren path taken
With little to promise
How did I even get here?
What did I miss?

A roof over my head
With food on the table
I was well-cared for
Few may dream of such a fable

Then why do I feel
That I'm not enough?
That I could've done more
Was I of harder stuff?

Lord Brahma, may I dare?
To imagine alternative creations
Where I'm a reliable son
And cause for my family's celebrations

Mr. Sagan, may I dare?
To visualise a world
Where I'm a practitioner of science
And I see singularities unfurled

O Cupid, may I dare?
To picture a quaint life

One in which I never lost a friend
And my sweetheart is my wife

Ah yes, my foolish measure
Has had unfruitful consequences
But no point in crying over spilled milk
Perhaps I need a new set of lenses

And that's when I remember Kintsugi
A Nipponese's way to repair broken pottery
Believe he, every tear in your soul
A playwright's act in your life's story

And so, if I can't be a candle
I declare I'll be the mirror
Indeed, a road less glamorous
But it would absolutely be my pleasure.

About Ronak Shah

Ronak Shah is a writer, music artist and visual-novel producer from Mumbai. He dreams to combine his writing skills with his penchant for physics to spread the awe of science. He is the author of the poetry anthology 'In Search of Starlight'. You can visit his website here: https://ronakshah.me

Burn them to Ashes

Saba Mirza. F

Bits of paper hold your worth,
Stuffed purse
Defines your worth.

Greedily,
Sweets and guests
Sneak in.

But
When you are broke,
Even simple words are venom.
Hearts break,
Relationships snap
No friends remain,
Only foes.

Nobody cares how you feel,
Shattered
Stabbed
But cannot speak.
Remember, 'You are broke.'

Bring the bits of paper that made us corpses,
Burn them to ashes
For
They cannot say my worth.

About Saba Mirza. F

Saba Mirza. F is a student pursuing M.A in English at the University of Madras. Inspired by everyday experiences, she weaves emotions into simple, crisp poetry that connects with readers. She continues to grow as a poet, crafting with an economy of words to create powerful effects.

Sunday Mornings

Satyapriya Pal

It's a Sunday morning,
I can't get up, I can't sleep in.
The birds are far too loud.

The covers are heavy on my skin,
But it's far too cold to get rid of them.

Could it be, that *you*-
You are what I am missing?
Another person to share this warmth,
This bed, these covers, and my heart with?

Would your breathy voice drown the birds'?
Could I possibly forget petrichor, just to love the
smell of you?

Would this feeling go away?
If my Sunday mornings were shared with you?

About Satyapriya Pal

Satyapriya Pal is an undergraduate student who
enjoys both science and creative expression. She
writes poetry about everyday moments and

emotions. When not studying, she spends time crocheting or listening to music. Her work is a way to capture thoughts that might otherwise go unsaid.

At Evening

Satya Sanjivan Nayak

Let me now watch you.
Why only the mirror aches
In your tenderness? Let me,
Too, into the folds of the saree.
This joy is free, separate, and unequal.

I don't mind the minutes.
Love demands time
And the stony border
Of your classic red saree
Is unreplicable. *Go ahead.*

Sit at your mahogany dresser
Like myna perched on your guava tree
Unseen in the cool rustling leaves
And screech at my reflection,
Turn your brown body and its rounded wings
And confirm your little black *tikli.*

I am alone with these lines,
A steady image of you occupies them,
Which you cannot see.
The facts are plain:
You are dearer than love
More present, more vocal to my soul.
Now take me into your arms.

About Satya Sanjivan Nayak

Satya Sanjivan Nayak is an aspiring poet and novelist from India. He completed his Masters in English Literature from Ravenshaw University, Cuttack. He has published poems in "Otherwise Engaged A Literature and Arts Journal" Volume 13 (Summer 2024) and "EKL REVIEW" Issue 11 (August 2024).

Oh, to be loved!

Sharmeen Ali

Oh, to be loved!
Oh, to be touched!
Oh, to be cared for!

Oh, to be loved!
To have someone who caresses your head
As you lie upon his lap,
Your mind swirling with deep, tormenting thoughts.
To have someone who loves you
Irrespective of the small imperfections of yours.

Oh, to be touched!
To have someone whose touch soothes you,
Taking away your pain and insecurities,
Embracing you in warmth,
Shielding you from the world's negativity.

Oh, to be cared for!
To have someone beside you on days
When nothing feels right—
When you are curled in pain, lost in echoes of the
past.
Someone who cares for you
Like a child lost in a trance.

Oh, to be comforted!
To hear sweet whispers in your ear
To be adored for the smallest things—
Your likes, your dislikes,
And all that makes you, *you*.

Oh, to be embraced!
To have someone who showers you
With kisses and hugs,
Even before you ask,
Holding you tightly,
Infusing you with warmth.

Oh, to be seen!
To be the only one in his eyes amidst a sea of faces.
For him to see beyond appearances,
Recognizing your soul and loving it just the same.
To seek only you,
To gaze with unwavering love and respect.

Oh, to be needed!
To have someone who keeps his promises,
Whose devotion never wavers.
To have someone who kneels before you,
Sealing the vow with trust.

Oh, to be married!
To build a life together, brick by brick,
Turning a house into a home.
Filling it with warmth, laughter, and dreams.
To know that through every storm,
He will stand by you, unwavering.

Oh, to be cherished!
To have someone stand by you
Through morning sickness or sorrow.
A rock that never stumbles,
His eyes filled with the same love
That first saw you.

Oh, to be together!
To hold his hand until your final breath.
To share laughter and smiles,
Even when you have the toothless grin of age.
To take your last breath in his arms,
Knowing his love gave meaning to your existence.

Oh, to be truly loved!

About Sharmeen Ali

Sharmeen Ali is 24 years old and holds a Master's degree in English Literature. Passionate about literature, she explores themes of love, identity and human emotions through poetry. This anthology marks her first published work, and she hopes to continue sharing her words with the world.

Crimson Verses

Suhani Patil

For me,
peace sounds like,
the sound of blood, dripping on the pages,
I am bleeding, through my eyes, ears, nose,
the pages start becoming red,
soaking up my agonies,
taking the form of ink on papers.

And as the crimson stains the lines,
the pages cradle my anguish,
every drop, every word,
weaving my torment into poetry.

With each verse,
the weight eases,
until my pain, no longer mine,
lives quietly in the ink.

A story I've survived.

About Suhani Patil

Suhani Patil is a second-year student from
Kolhapur, Maharashtra. Though she studies science,

poetry and literature is where she truly finds her voice. She started writing last year, and it has become her only way of expressing emotions she struggles to say aloud. With 72 poems so far, this is her journey. This poem is her attempt to capture what poetry means to her.

Our Incomplete Story

Sumit Ganguli

*The last poetic conversation between
Ladylove/Paramour (Female-Lover) and
Beau/Heartbreaker (Male-Lover).*

Both were sitting on a bench in a small park which
is located near their home, keeping their hands on
each other. Lady love tilted her head on Beau's
shoulder for more comfort and love. As the day
started to roll on, the time for them together started
to diminish. Both knew each other from their
college days. The moment was very sad even nature
felt it. The leaves were falling from the trees, the
bushes were rubbing against each other in such a
way that it could catch fire. A sudden strong wind
blew and took the leaves away. It seemed a storm is
going to hit the park and it felt that nature itself
don't want their separation…

*Paramour
(Female lover)*

Many people left me alone,
You are the one who broke me completely,
You are the one who gave me reasons to live,
Dreams whatever I have woven been taken too far.
My favourite star is gone forever.

You never know how painful it is,
Keeping those moments in my and your heart
forever,
You left behind every memory I loved.

Your departure made my breathing painful,
Many of your words were the reasons for my smile.
What do I say Now?
Now even my smile has become a crime.

Many people came and went.
But your leaving broke me
Now, I am going to marry someone,
for family's wishes…
But, how hard it is for me you don't know,
But remember my soul will belong to you,
And will remain yours forever…

Yes, I will meet definitely
After death, where the concepts of wrong doings
And right doings do not meet between the
mountains of
peace…We will meet in the mountains!

Beau
(Male Lover)

There is no more peace left anymore,
I meet with other people like I used to before,
Your love is gone but one-sided stayed with me,
My moon is gone forever.

You were the ocean and I the sky,
Or perfectly matched just like the two sides of
magnet,
I am the faded flower of the garden now,
Somewhere beyond the horizon we will meet.

But the moon is safe from the storms of the sun,
And the tides touch the horizons with its waves,
Now, it's just a poison
Needs to be consumed from the Lake of Nectar.

The love for you will stay in my heart,
Just like the fire in the Immortal flame.
The pain cannot be explained,
But from tears can be understood.
Love life has never been easy so far,
Small quarrels to long promises.

Now I will try my best not to get attached to
anyone,
In my entire lifetime.

For all it's turmoil of life
I want you to meet me in the mountains of peace,
Where the concepts of Wrong doings & Right
doings don't meet…
Will you meet me there?

After this, they said their final goodbyes to each
other with lots of pain and tears. Paramour married
and stayed busy with her life. Although not happy,

but she accepted her faith and walked on the designed path by God. On the other hand, Beau never married; he stayed single and changed the city where he used to live and waited for Paramour's return in his life. He adopted two kids and taught them the real meaning of love. He knew that Paramour wouldn't return but still there was a little 1% hope for which he stayed single all his life. And in the end, life went on and with it, people kept getting separated. Who knows how many stories kept getting created and printed in the books, how many people died and how many stories got lost? A quote from famous Urdu poet explains everything about what love is and what incompleteness in love is:

 "Ab ke hum bichhde to shaayad kabhi khwaabon mein milein, jis tarah sookhe hue phool kitaabon mein milein."

("If we part now, we might meet in dreams, like dried flowers found in old books.")
~ Ahmad Faraz

About Sumit Ganguli

Sumit Ganguli is a poet from Durgapur, West Bengal. His journey began with 'Father's Love' in 'The Language of Love' anthology. Inspired by literary giants, he explores the complexities of love and seeks understanding in the artistic world.

Small Gestures, Big Smiles

S. Tejaswini

Woman, a delicate yet elegant masterpiece,
In the tapestry of Life, she's a vital part.
Her eyes sparkle like a star when in happiness,
And her eyes tear up like drops when in sadness.

A woman, a soul of depth, where feelings reside,
She overthinks, cares and forgives too easily.
She wonders if anyone truly thinks as deeply as she
does,
The soul of a woman, a treasure trove!

Woman and her happiness, when a man shows
chivalry,
His small gestures light up her face.
A gentle touch and a warm kiss on her forehead,
Make her feel as home during storms.

A woman and her happiness—
When someone tracks her dates,
When someone cares for her during her periods,
When someone pampers her with effort and food.
It's the smallest things that brighten her mood
cycle.

Woman and her happiness, when someone asks out,
For an ice-cream or a plate of *panipuri,*
She melts and bursts with the flavors of joy,

It's the smallest things that brighten her mood.

A woman's happiness, unbound—
When she spots her favourite earrings on the
roadside, or
When she finds a dress that fits her perfectly.
It's the smallest things that make her happy.

A woman's happiness is profusely found when,
Even efforts are made in a simpler way.
It's her, she is a woman,
Who finds joy even in the smallest gestures.

About S.Tejaswini

S. Tejaswini, a young and aspiring writer in her
early twenties, recently graduated with a degree in
English Literature. Her creative talents have been
recognized through the publication of her poem in
the anthology 'The Language of Love'. She has also
taken part in a creative writing workshop, where her
work was featured in the event souvenir, and has
presented scholarly papers at five national
conferences and one in an international conference.
A heart full of love, Tejaswini finds joy in capturing
her emotions and dreams through the art of poetry.
For feedbacks: @s02_poetry

About The Literary Mosaic

'The Literary Mosaic' is the third anthology project by authors Abhishek Thakkar and Purba Chakraborty who are also the compilers and editors of the book. Their first two poetry projects 'The Language of Love' and 'The Language of Divinity received roaring success and gained a lot of accolades from the literary fraternity. Abhishek and Purba, hailing from two states of India, Gujarat and West Bengal respectively have been in a long-distance relationship for six years before tying the knot in 2023.

After the success of 'The Language of Love' and 'The Language of Divinity', they decided to bring a book of poems and short stories that will echo the diverse voices of writers. This open-themed anthology features poems and short stories of various flavours by forty talented Indian writers and poets.

They also plan to launch many more poetry and short story projects in the near future so that they can provide a platform to many talented poets and writers whose voice need to be heard.
If you enjoyed reading this book, kindly leave a review on Amazon and Instagram.

You can also send your feedback or review at
theliterarymosaic@gmail.com
You can get in touch with them on Instagram at
@abhishekvthakkar1010 and @purba_chakraborty

COMPILED & EDITED
BY
ABHISHEK THAKKAR &
PURBA CHAKRABORTY
THE
LANGUAGE
OF LOVE
A bouquet of soulful love poems

COMPILED & EDITED
BY
ABHISHEK THAKKAR &
PURBA CHAKRABORTY
THE
LANGUAGE
OF DIVINITY
A bouquet of spiritual poems

You can grab a copy of 'The Language of Love' and 'The Language of Divinity' on Amazon.

www.ingramcontent.com/pod-product-compliance
Lightning Source LLC
Chambersburg PA
CBHW031145130726
47988CB00006B/2544